Enchantment

poems by

Karen Leahy

Finishing Line Press
Georgetown, Kentucky

Enchantment

ACKNOWLEDGMENTS

An earlier version of Rising appeared in my memoir, *The Summer of Yes: An
Ex-Nun's Story.*

Abundant thanks are due the many people who so graciously helped bring
this book to press:

Zoya Korol of Kyiv for permission to use the elegant cover image; Camilla
Golden, graphic designer and friend, for her help with cover design; Ella
and Veronica Stern, for author photographs, as well as promotion and
PR advice; Thomas Moore, for the use of the opening quote; Cathleen
O'Connell and Marylou Streznewski, for their generous words; teachers,
mentors, friends, and family who cheered me on; the staff of Finishing Line
Press; and the many poets whose gorgeous lines made me long to be in their
company.

Publisher: Leah Huete de Maines
Editor: Christen Kincaid
Cover Art: Zoya Korol
Author Photo: Veronica Stern
Cover Design: Camilla Golden, Camillart.com

Order online: www.finishinglinepress.com
also available on amazon.com

Author inquiries and mail orders:
Finishing Line Press
PO Box 1626
Georgetown, Kentucky 40324
USA

Contents

This book is dedicated to my father, James Leahy,
who gave me my first book of poetry
and who was easily enchanted.

"The soul has an absolute, unforgiving need
for regular excursions into enchantment."
Thomas Moore: "The Re-enchantment of Everyday Life"

On the Seine

The boat simply
gives in to the current.
Whatever power is
easing us downstream in the dark
draws no attention
to itself, as though the ocean
beckons
          from three days away
                    and the boat obeys.

We pass under
the last of the city's bridges,
each light-span
less ornate at this
modest end of Paris,
a few lamps still lit
in houseboat windows.
          Deeper darkness and quiet
                    draw us on.

Alone on the front deck, I
succumb to the opiate pace,
to the fragrance
of mid-summer magnified
by the dark,
this river journey
unfolding
          like a hushed nocturne,
                    and I a part of it,

existing
for this hour
in the same key
          as the river
                    and the night.

Close Encounter

I'm heading into the market; he's coming out.
He's 20-something, cute & capped &
striding, his young energy
delicious, and I'm the old lady he could ignore,
not see, and I would be ok with that,
not needing his attention.
      But in those few seconds,
he makes eye contact, and
smiles, really smiles, and I smile back
and walk on with a handful of happiness.

Enchantment

Bemoaning November's waning light, forgetting
what gifts larger darkness can bring,
we relinquish the cafe's warmth and
brace against the night's wintry wind.
But look: there reigns the late autumn moon, the
Frost Moon, full and fabulous, a silver sign
of happiness. Clouds unravel from the west and
dance past their cool queen,
happy children of the night, their energy
infectious, so we mortals disregard concerns
fastened to us like old tin cans
and let ourselves feel the
moan of pleasure from the earth's core. Tonight,
we're light on our feet again. We laugh
deep laughs and store away this
bright delight against darknesses to come.

The Hours, Late Winter

Matins

Outside the window,
snow silences morning.
A small orchid beside me on the table
for company, its vivid color
quiet in the predawn light.
Fruit bowl, soft white table cloth,
stillness.
That is everything.

Lauds

Winter-jacket-weather still, but
air whispers Spring,
woos snow into retreat.
Drinking coffee outdoors
on the low stone wall,
viewing-stand for the show
a venerable magnolia
puts on each year, this tree
the only one around
with buds—almond-sized now
but six quick weeks
is all she needs
before letting loose
the profligate beauty
of a thousand hand-sized
hurrahs.

Vespers

Dark, drizzly night.
Surprise: against an entrance light, the sparkle
of raindrops set aglow all along the undersides
of black branches, such tiny, perfect pearls
you stop, keys in hand and chill forgotten,
for this wee blessing.
You must see. You must honor this beauty.

For a few seconds as you near
your front door, the miracle
of being a sentient being with sight and soul
sweeps you up in a grand hymn of praise.

So let the whole choir of
lindens and dogwoods and holly bushes
and glistening grass and raindrops
and incense of evening air
say
Amen.

July Night, Frosty Drew Observatory

One luminous night, moonless,
the Rhode Island air as lovely as air can be,
we wait on the grass as true dark
    settles down around us.

    Quiet voices rise—a child's treble,
lovers' murmurs. We wait and watch from
here on our home planet, and slowly
    we begin to see:

    Venus, Mars, a few bright stars—
Arcturus, Vega, the Pleiades—then slowly,
more stars,   and more,   and more until
    an epiphany of bright worlds

    gleams
from horizon to horizon against a black sky.
Against the whole, wild Milky Way and its
ancient worlds of dense matter, gases, minerals,
unseen forces,
    against

    all that whirls,
expands, contracts, explodes, regathers,
against its beckoning mysteries and majesty,
                here am I.

    I exist in this immensity
beyond time, beyond care. I know the preciousness
of this hour, the humor
of my beautiful insignificance,
    and I laugh out loud.

    We are made
of the same stuff as the stars. I carry the resonance
of this night in my earthly breath and bones
for the brilliant blink of cosmic time that is
    a human life.

A Three-Year-Old Eats Strawberries

She plays quietly in the kitchen,
coming in without fanfare
to be with Momma. You hardly notice
how many times she crosses to the blue bowl
full of strawberries and returns
to the low stool beside her mother.

The next time you do notice:
how she holds a strawberry to her mouth
with both hands, the way a squirrel would,
gnawing at the delicious fruit
with total, sloppy attention
till red juice runs down between tiny fingers.

If the Strawberry Growers' Association
could get this on camera!—
or Buddhist monks who teach
mindful eating. This child
makes you want to taste a strawberry right now
as though you were three years old.

Window Seat

Our flight takes us over the beautiful bones
of mountains, winter-whitened for centuries.
   Hills hold back and let the valley be,
      circle it, stand guard with all their inner power
      in a gesture of generosity, allowing
   inhabitants of the valley to touch
the skin of the earth.

From my window seat on a cross-country flight
   west to Portland, I become an explorer, enthralled
      by what opens below me. A little further north,
      foothills amble along, creased and wrinkled
      like old skin over knuckle bones. Though I see
   no central river, inventive waterways
salamander in all directions.

On land in days to come, I will study
   the topography of the region in maps
      made by earlier explorers worthy of that title
      and surmise that we crossed near
   Navajo Mountain, Utah. The name fits
   these ancient land forms and my sense
that they are sacred.

We fly further north and west. Here
   the land relaxes into low hills.
      Smooth arms of water, arrayed
         in aquas and greens, snuggle
      all around, this canvas only visible
   from a vantage point the first explorers
never dreamed of, but which I,

through no virtue of my own,
   am blessed with today because a computer
      at the airport gave me
a window seat.

In Praise of the Quilters of Gee's Bend, Alabama

Lillie Mae Pettway,
we never met, but today your
bold-colored quilt speaks to me.

Old patterns we love—
checks, dots, florals, stripes and stars—
quilting's poetry.

Skilled hands of women
play fast and loose with quilt form,
sewing in free verse.

A lineage up from slavery
and Jim Crow, using scraps
to fashion warmth and sisterhood.

A quilt is language
needing no dictionary,
telling women's lives.

Blind Contour Drawing at Starbuck's

Wet winter morning calls for serious coffee, steaming, favorite back corner table. Paper and pen poised for poetry, I watch. Old codger in crumpled cap over by the window. That profile. My hand starts drawing without looking down, without lifting the pen, something tried at a workshop somewhere. A few seconds and there he is, taking up a quarter of the only sheet of paper I brought to write poetry on. But I like it. He's younger, livelier on the page.

One more?—that woman waiting for her order, nice face.... Ooh. Sorry, Miss. You came out a crone. But what character! That chin! A don't-mess-with-me kind of look.

Ok, I get it. Override the bossy brain and *bingo*!—cubism marries cartoon, of no consequence whatsoever except getting out of my own way, playing around, watching out of the corner of my eye for any creative spark that might fly up. Say, here's the day, the reality before you, and you just trust that your years have given you enough to go on so you don't need to boss yourself around. Just keeping an eye out for the good stuff.

Lean back. At lukewarm, good coffee is more interesting, heat not hiding flavor, and I am a happy duck, back here in my corner, in love now with a nasty day and with inspiration coming slant.

An Artist Walks into a Jazz Joint
after a painting by LaShun Beal

An artist walks into a jazz joint. Piano keys stride
all over Basin Street and a Duke Ellington tune. A horn's wah-wah
heats it up, and the bass fiddle grunts its approval.

There's a woman—there's always a woman—as slinky as a
slide trombone and as perfect as the calla lily beside her.
The artist simply must translate this scene into color—

shameless red, scorching orange, a deep and dangerous blue, the
eternal drama of black and white, and a gold you can't resist. He is
overcome with curves—the seductive

arch of the lily, the mouth of the horn, a wine glass, the woman's
bare shoulder, her breast, her hip, the bass fiddle inspired by those hips.
And he can't help himself: he curves the line of piano keys till

they glide away, growing smaller like a road twisting out of sight.
An artist could get drunk on curves like these, so he takes some
straight lines to sober up, puts a smaller frame

inside the outer one, and stares long and hard at the bass fiddle's
straight neck. The horn, eager to help out, stands on its head and tries
to look tall. The artist even gives the woman

sharp features—jaw, nose--nothing very curvy there, as though
he's learned Don't mess with a dame!
One more stroke. There. Finished. He invites you in.

Debut, with Birds and Balloons

Sakura Park band shell. A flutist
  glances up at the birds and smiles.
Swallows sashay in and out of nests
  in the gazebo roof rafters, sing
in piccolo range, and carry on unbothered
  by the melodic chirps this gaggle
of large beings is sending up.

The young composer hears his untitled work
  for the first time. Birds don't have a line
in the score, but spice up his harmonies *ad libitum*.
  Throw in the great bell of Riverside Church
sounding the half hour just as the song approaches
  its final resting place, and you have
high and low notes he didn't think to write.

From across Riverside Drive, a gang
  of happy balloons waves to us.
Swallows, balloons, the great church bell,
  and a lyrical breeze
that weaves between the notes:
  a one-time-only performance of
Hymn to Serendipity.

Call Me Timothy

He knows my name, but today,
in the mystery of a toddler's mind,
he calls me by his. Again and again

he beckons me. I am a happy accomplice
in book-reading, block-building
(I'm a sucker for block-building),

giggling, snuggling. Could he
have decided that
I am really his?—I,

the honorary grandmother, his real ones
half a world away. I stood in for them
at his birth, and look:

so quickly he is three!
Firmly rooted in my heart,
no question he is mine.

Go ahead, beautiful boy,
call me Timothy.

Past Peak

After the weather report,
a fall foliage map, the whole Northeast
grayed out, Maine through Pennsylvania, and deeper
into Virginia, North Carolina, Tennessee.
"Past peak" says the legend.
Fall foliage, the glory we think of
when we think of Vermont's acres of
gold, vermillion, peach, and
a rainbow of shades between—
past peak now. Sorry folks. If you didn't
pay attention....

But then

you go out, and the trees that have
held on and defied the peak
beckon to you, their singular beauty
more visible to weary eyes. See
how that Japanese maple, backlit by sun,
commands the hill, dazzles in deep ruby and garnet,
queenly in autumn robes. Or the gang
of ginkos near the bagel shop shaking
their vivid leaf-fans and showering
high yellowness all around.
I'll take *past peak* every time.
I am, too—past peak—but my show
isn't over either.

Say It!

Say it quietly: *amethyst*,
and the mystery of its centuries-long making
lies before you. Sit up straight when you summon
Pythagoras, pith-helmeted, ready
to mine *isosceles* triangles
for the greater good.

Or call upon the mime,
onomatopoeia, and you might
snooker him into adding some
shazam to your lines.
And ah! oh! *avocado!*
Feel it: so smooth in the mouth.

My dear Uncle Dave taught
three-year-old me
the Marine Hymn. No idea
what it meant, but belted out
Mon-te-zoo-OO-ma
with that delicious extra oo.

That started it. I've never stopped
loving how some *oo* words tickle the ear, like
bamboozle, canoodle, even *oomph*.
And so many other yummy words to savor!
Go ahead, Open the dictionary and
raise a little *ruckus!*

Spring Fling

Weeping cherry tree, they call you, little tree,
and maybe you do look weepy in winter when
ice bends your branches down.
But today you seem ready to dance.
You're a tree in a blossomy pink tutu!

I have no doubt
that the mockingbird
reciting his *Poem to Spring*
in 22 borrowed birdsongs
is showing off for you.

I wouldn't be surprised
if you took a happy little turn
when no one was watching
(except, perhaps,
the mockingbird and me).

Being Alive

with a nod to e e cummings

                    I walk the long way round
to the farmer's market, morning air
bright and breathable and brushed with cool.
I take time to admire the pattern and
palette of produce stands, chat with vendors, accept
a sample of golden milk from the Indian spice seller—
turmeric, cumin, and saffron in hot almond milk—
a revelation.

                    On the way back,
I'm easily waylaid by the lure
of hot coffee and a chair outside the French bakery.
I watch a toddler solve the problem
of how to get off her chair without help
on her fourth try, her mother distracted, so
I give a silent cheer.

                    Over my head,
soothing greenness of leaves against
a true blue dream of sky
if I ever saw one. I wish Ginny and Cookie
were here with me, sipping coffee
in Earth's finest air. Why am I
the one still alive? At least
for this round, shining gift of a morning,
let me let it all in—for them.

In the Quiet

The refrigerator motor breathes out as it settles down
in the six a.m. silence. The day inhales,

leaning toward light. I wait, keep track as tree-tops go golden,
this side of the planet receiving its sun-gifts with silent gratitude.

Watching, writing, I feel unlikely here, almost accidental.
In the quiet, I sense a line to a faraway someone from centuries past—

an Irish monk, maybe—sitting in a dim room, keeping watch
at dawn, as I do, both of us honoring words

that fall out of silence onto the page.

love map

by unknown roads
my thoughts find their way
to your smile

Sitting Outdoors at the Café Le Monde
for John

Intent as ancient statesmen with history in their hands
we talk, our bodies close together in the wise September air
as we spin through space and time, feeling only
the calm of sun on our shoulders, then slowly shade, and
still we talk.

Several tables away a girl of nine or ten watches. I believe
she knows something beautiful is happening.
We are creating a new world order:
deciding to be lovers.

Tango

"Let the moon untangle itself from the clothesline…"
Antoinette Brim

Let the moon untangle itself
from the paparazzi clouds
and dance free on the silver sea.

Let the silver sea sing
in the tango rhythm of tides,
in the language of lovers.

Let us learn the language of lovers
with its passionate poetry
and sweet, sibilant kisses,

kisses that tonight
have the tang
of the silver sea in them

while the moon untangles itself
from the crowds of clouds
and dances free.

The Way He Moves

That's me,
      standing at the fence
      just outside the ice rink in Stuytown,
      unable to take my eyes off him—
      that gorgeous skater—how he
            leans deep
            into knife-swift turns,
laughing
      because gravity doesn't apply to him.
      Two small boys trying to catch him
      don't stand a chance,

      the shine
      of youth and winter sun on him,
      a glint of beautiful danger
      coming off that body,
      knowing he's on top of his game.

I don't give a fig
      about his character.
      I just want to watch him,
      to let myself be lured
      out of the
            tamped-down
            ordinary
      till I feel myself
      in the dance of it,
      his eloquent body
      having its way with the ice,
            the space,
                the light,
                    my pulse.

We could kid ourselves
      and say it's just about the aesthetics,
      But we know

exactly
what's going on.

It's like that warm evening
    more than half my life ago,
    I, a young nun, watching
    a visiting teacher play touch football
     with my high school boys.
    I was shocked to realize
    how much
    I enjoyed watching him—
    that same kind of male energy, the same
    mastery, grace, laughing at his prowess.
           (Within a year, I would
           walk out of the convent.
           And yes,
           I did see him again.)

I laugh at myself now. I haven't changed.
    I'm a sucker for a man who moves well.
    I believe I actually fell in love with my husband
    just watching him
    walk down the street:
    that   long   easy   stride
    I never stopped loving
    and just enough cockiness
    to up the ante.

I find myself on First Avenue, and
    I must be smiling because
    a younger woman glances up and smiles at me.
   Sweetheart,
    this is the way an older woman looks
    when she lets a gorgeous man
    remind her
          she's not dead yet.

Neighborhood

"It ain't home... Until somehow yer soul is sort o' wrapped around everything."
   Edgar Guest

I know the same town-crier crow will announce at 5:45 a.m. that the day has officially begun.

I know which of the two little girls in the apartment below is crying.

I know the circle of wise linden trees in the courtyard, and they know me.

I know how the mandevilla flowers in front of Bacio Ristorante drink in light and give back color so rich and red you can almost taste it.

I know how my oldest neighbor walks on her daily rounds, her arms bent and elbows slightly back, bird-like.

I know the setting sun will stall over the gas station long enough to find my living room window and leave a blessing inside.

I see now how this place, where I thought I was just perching for a while, is home.

Rising

I walk among trees in my father's yard, some doubled in size
since he tended them, the yard his small paradise. He took as
blessing all blooms and berries—dogwood, flowering crab,
mountain ash. His purple beech stands in somber glory with
wide, paternal reach.

He knew the habits of every burrowing thing that nested and
nibbled on the edges of his yard. And there: weather-worn
bird feeder where he welcomed one and all: cardinal, nuthatch,
a bright flash of yellow finch; mourning doves who hung around,
grieving; now and then the pride of a pileated woodpecker.

Evening comes down now, easy and cool. Colors dim; fragrance
floats up—musk of earth, tang of grass. My mother
will move soon. When the house is sold, where will I go
to feel my father's presence? Molecules of his breath, his joy,
are woven into the bark and carried on the fragrant air.

I run my hand down the weathered shank of the beech tree.
Fireflies—so many tonight!—rise glowing from the grass,
small, silent celebrations of his spirit, rising everywhere and
signing to me, *Nothing of a father's love is ever lost.*

Souvenir

If I were allowed to take
one perfect human moment from
here to the other side of death,
what would I choose? Would it be
Katie's smile?—the smile
I do nothing to deserve except
let her beauty reflect back to her,
marveling then, and even now, that
a two-year-old can give off
such radiance.

Or driving through the wild, high
heaven-scape of Big Sur
in a yellow convertible: the
champagne air, the coast
hurrying down to the sea, to waves that
flash their energy, swoop in,
burble with liquid laughter. And
I laugh, too, and shout, because
how else can you respond
to such a day?

How to choose from among
life's incandescent moments?
Ah! Of course. What I can't bear
to leave behind:
lying beside you, whom I love,
your body curled against mine, the
half-waking when you turn, so that
I turn to fit you and,
in the cozy darkness of night,
my whole body smiles.

That.

Karen Leahy is the author of a memoir, *The Summer of Yes: An Ex-Nun's Story*, which won the Benjamin Franklin Award for memoir from the Independent Book Publishers Association, as well as finalist medals in both memoir and women's issues from the Next Generation Indie Book Awards. Poems of hers have been published in two collections of writings about illness from Fairview Press and in several anthologies.

For some years, Karen was the proprietor of The StoryWeaver, writing short biographies of seniors to leave as legacies for their children and grandchildren. A former teacher of high school English and college music, Karen more recently received grants to lead writing workshops at two public libraries. She founded and led "The Writers' Club" at a senior living facility, sharing the writings at festive bi-annual events for all residents and families.

She has always loved words and writing, attempting in third grade to write a mystery story with two friends and winning a 7th-grade poetry contest. When writing the poem "The Hours," this line came to her: "You must stop; you must honor this beauty," and she realized she has felt this since early childhood. Only half a life later did she begin to express this in poetry.

Raised in Ohio as one of 10 children, Karen now lives in the New York area. She is a member of the International Women's Writing Guild.

www.ingramcontent.com/pod-product-compliance
Lightning Source LLC
Chambersburg PA
CBHW022058080426
42734CB00009B/1408